IN A PICKLE ØVER PANDAS

Written by
Melanie S. Weiss, RN

Illustrated by
Thomas Barnett

In A Pickle Over PANDAS
Copyright ©2015 Melanie S. Weiss

ISBN 978-1622-879-25-0 HARD COVER
ISBN 978-1622-879-23-6 PAPBERBACK
ISBN 978-1622-879-24-3 EBOOK

LCCN 2015942025

May 2015

Published and Distributed by
First Edition Design Publishing, Inc.
P.O. Box 20217, Sarasota, FL 34276-3217
www.firsteditiondesignpublishing.com

This book is not intended as a substitute for the medical advice of physicians. The reader should regularly consult a physician in matters relating to his/her health and particularly with respect to any symptoms that may require diagnosis or medical attention.

Dedication

This book is dedicated to all of the children around the globe afflicted by PANDAS/PANS and the doctors trying to help them.

I would like to thank my family and my sister, Alison Meyer, who supported me in writing this book, for her words of wisdom and gift of writing herself, and for leading me to Diana Pohlman.

I especially want to thank Diana Pohlman, *the* top mother, researcher, and crusader for PANDAS/PANS.

I would also like to thank all of the moms who I have communicated with via phone and those who have contacted me via e-mail from around the globe, including the United States, Canada, Europe, and Dubai, UAE, and of course their children.

Thank you!

Foreword

"Pandas" is a word that almost all children recognize as those lovable bamboo-eating gentle black-and-white bears from China. But to parents who are familiar with the disorder PANDAS, the word evokes terror. PANDAS, and its relative PANS, refer to a newly-recognized condition whereby previously normal children undergo a dramatic change in behavior (OCD, anxiety and tics, among other symptoms). Many parents can point to the very hour that their children changed. In some cases, the bacteria that causes the common "strep throat" seems responsible, but there are many other causes as well.

As a doctor who has treated over 3,000 patients with PANDAS/PANS since the late 1990's, I have come to appreciate the broad range of psychiatric and neurologic symptoms that can be associated with this chameleon of a disorder. We are beginning to find predisposing genes and develop animal models for the disorder, and prospects for better rational treatments seem very bright. In my opinion PANDAS/PANS is the vanguard of "the New Psychiatry," where we begin to find actual medical causes of psychiatric illness.

Melanie Weiss has written a little book that explains, in simple terms that children can understand, what PANDAS is all about. This is one of the very first such books written for children with PANDAS. Many children with PANDAS are as terrified as their parents as they struggle with a condition over which they feel helpless. I sincerely hope that this book will empower these children and their parents as they deal with PANDAS.

Rosario Trifiletti, MD, PhD
Child Neurology

Author's Note

PANDAS is an acronym for **P**ediatric **A**utoimmune **N**europsychiatric **D**isorder **A**ssociated with **S**treptococcus. This neurological disorder can initially affect children from the age of three to puberty, and sometimes beyond. More boys than girls become afflicted with this disorder at a ratio of approximately 2:1 to 3:1. Strep bacteria prompt dysfunctional antibodies to invade the basal ganglia of the brain, instead of fighting the strep itself. This results in a plethora of unusual and alarming symptoms. In addition to strep, bacteria such as mycoplasma and Lyme, and viruses fall under the new umbrella term, PANS, which is an acronym for **P**ediatric **A**cute-onset **N**europsychiatric **S**yndrome. Other disorders that may stem from PANDAS/PANS are Obsessive Compulsive Disorder (OCD), Tourette's Syndrome (TS), Oppositional Defiant Disorder (ODD), Attention Deficit Hyperactivity Disorder (ADHD), and Common Variable Immune Deficiency (CVID). It is important to note that PANDAS/PANS have dramatic and acute onsets, which differentiates them from the disorders mentioned above. A delay in proper diagnosis and treatment can rob the child of their childhood. Quick intervention with the appropriate antibiotic for an appropriate course of treatment is paramount in halting this disorder.

I woke up one morning and nothing felt right! I was scared but I didn't know why and couldn't really explain it to my parents. I felt worried and nervous. Then, I started crying and couldn't stop.

I was eight and a half years old and I did not want to go to school! I sat in my mom's lap and stayed very close to her whenever she left the room because it felt like something bad was going to happen. She held me close and sang lullabies and Christmas carols. This made me feel a little better. But, I knew something was still really wrong.

Was I going crazy? Why was God letting this happen to me? I had a lot of questions but no real answers. My mom had questions too, so she took me to the doctor. Then, we saw a lot more doctors to try to find out what was wrong. Boy, was I sick of going to doctors!

The doctors asked a bunch of questions, examined me, and took blood from my arm and put it into different tubes. Finally, one of the doctors said he knew what was wrong. He said I had *PANDAS*. The only pandas I knew of were the black and white bears I had seen at the zoo.

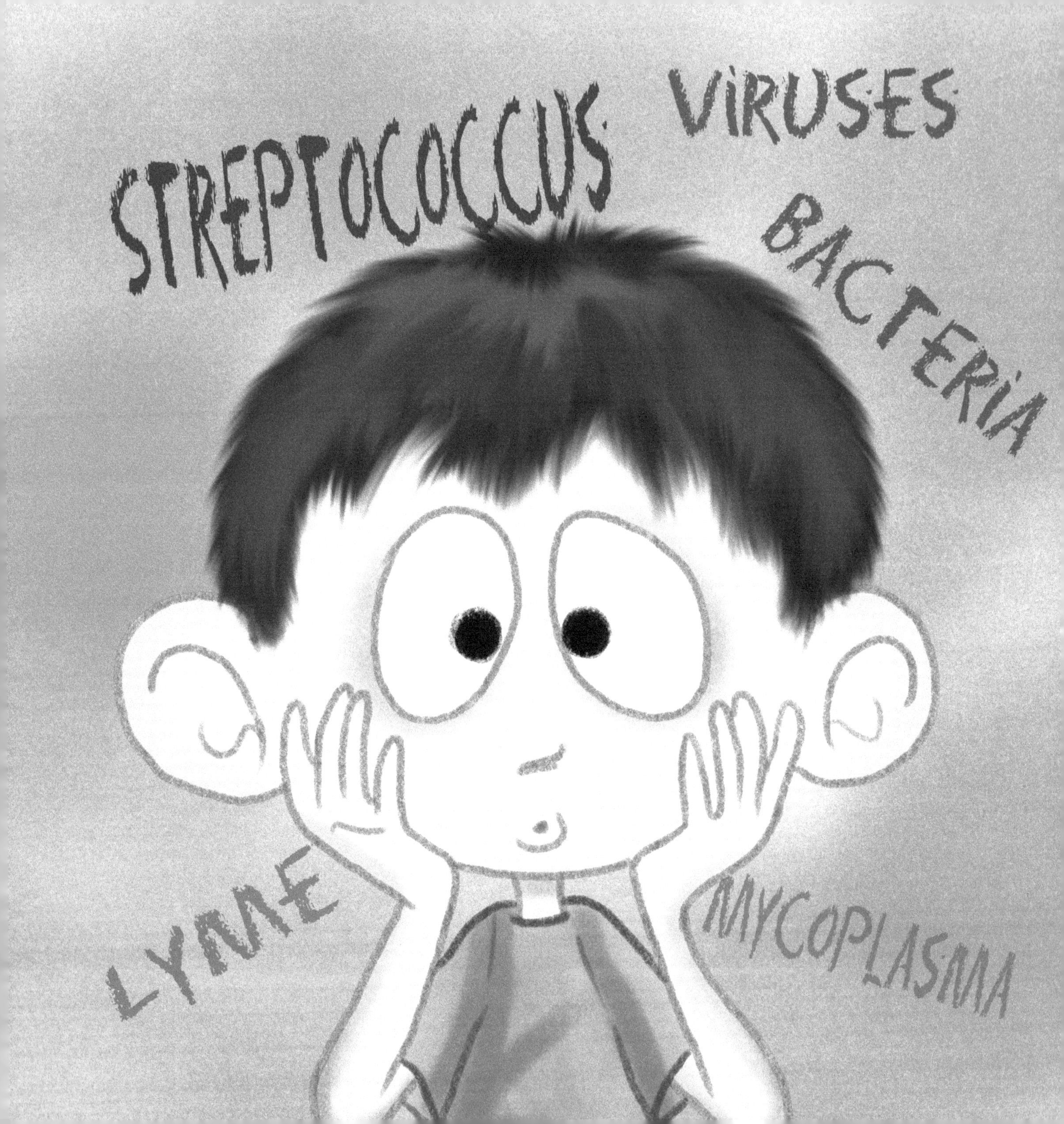
STREPTOCOCCUS
VIRUSES
BACTERIA
LYME
MYCOPLASMA

But, the doctor said this was different. The letters stand for a medical disorder that kids can get from bacteria called *streptococcus* or strep throat.

Usually, you get a really bad sore throat, fever, and maybe a belly ache. But, sometimes you don't. I never got any of those things that are called *symptoms*.

There are other *bacteria*, called *mycoplasma* and *Lyme*, and *viruses* that can cause this disorder too. A newer name for the disorder is *PANS*.

I was just glad they figured out what was wrong and that I was not going crazy.

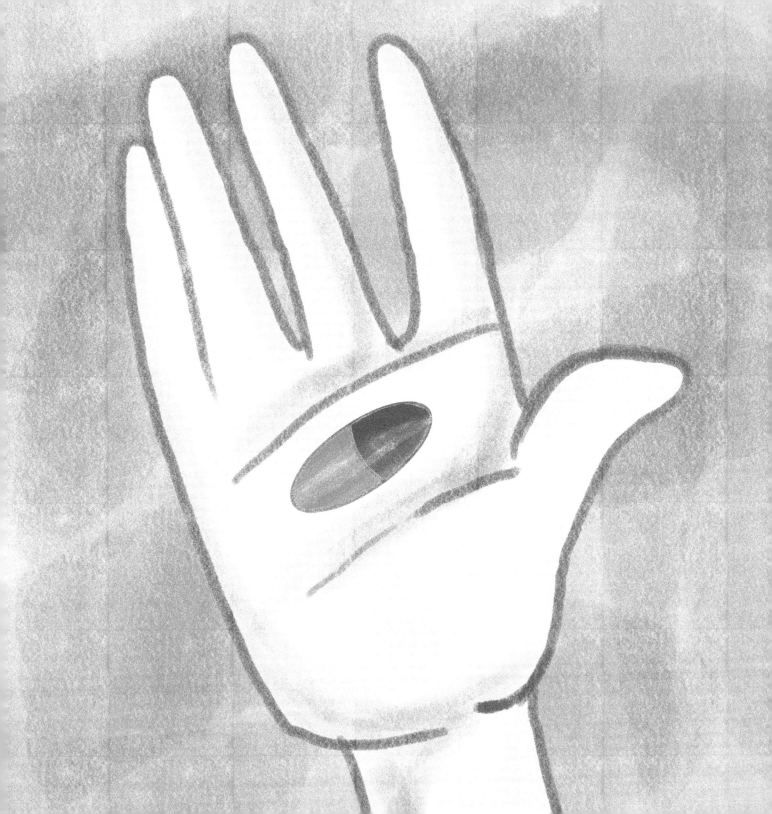

When you get those symptoms, the doctor gives you medicine you swallow, called an *antibiotic*. In a few days you feel better.

When you don't get those symptoms or your *throat culture* is negative (which may not be true), you don't get the antibiotic and that's when things can get all screwy.

As time passes without treatment with an antibiotic, more problems may start happening.

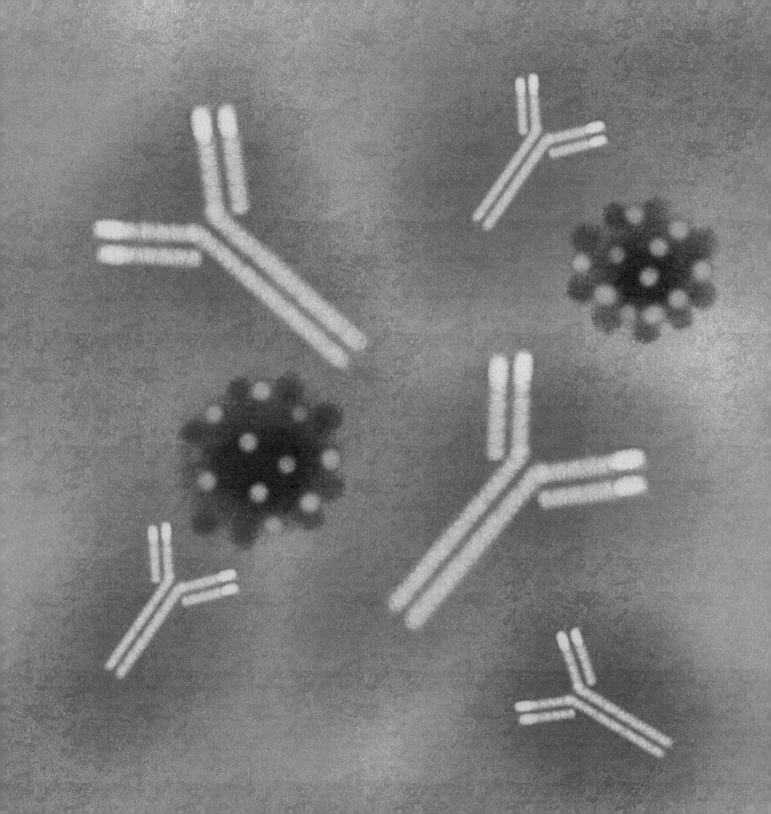

Our bodies make something called *antibodies* to fight bacterial illnesses, like strep throat, that can make us sick. In some kids, the antibodies don't fight the bacteria like they should but attack our own body instead. When the antibodies behave like this, it's called an *autoimmune* response.

The *immune system* inside our body is supposed to protect us from germs and keep us healthy. When it's not working right, we can get sick and get lots of symptoms.

I started getting headaches and stomach aches. I just didn't feel well and my mom said I looked pale all the time. Then, some really strange stuff started happening.

I started getting some bad thoughts about things and couldn't get them out of my head no matter how hard I tried. The thoughts scared me and made me even more nervous.

When you're really nervous all the time the doctors call it *anxiety*. Going on the computer or playing video games really helped take my mind off of the bad thoughts.

Then, for some strange reason, I began having to repeat doing things I had done already. I knew it didn't make sense to keep doing things over and over, but I just couldn't stop. Something was making me do it and I didn't understand why.

The doctors call these strange symptoms *Obsessive Compulsive Disorder or OCD*. This happens all because your antibodies aren't working right.

Some kids even get tics, a sign of *Tourette's Syndrome* or TS. Tics are when you keep moving your head a certain way, keep making sounds in your throat, or say things you don't mean without any control over it.

Some strange and embarrassing things can happen that you have no control over. Some kids even wet the bed while sleeping at night. I wasn't sleeping very well and I didn't really want to eat much.

Sometimes, I would get really angry and have tantrums. My teacher said my handwriting was getting worse and I was having some trouble with math. I didn't have that much trouble with math before.

It was hard getting through a whole day at school. I felt restless and the kids were noticing some of the repetitive things I was doing, like touching the closet door in the classroom over and over.

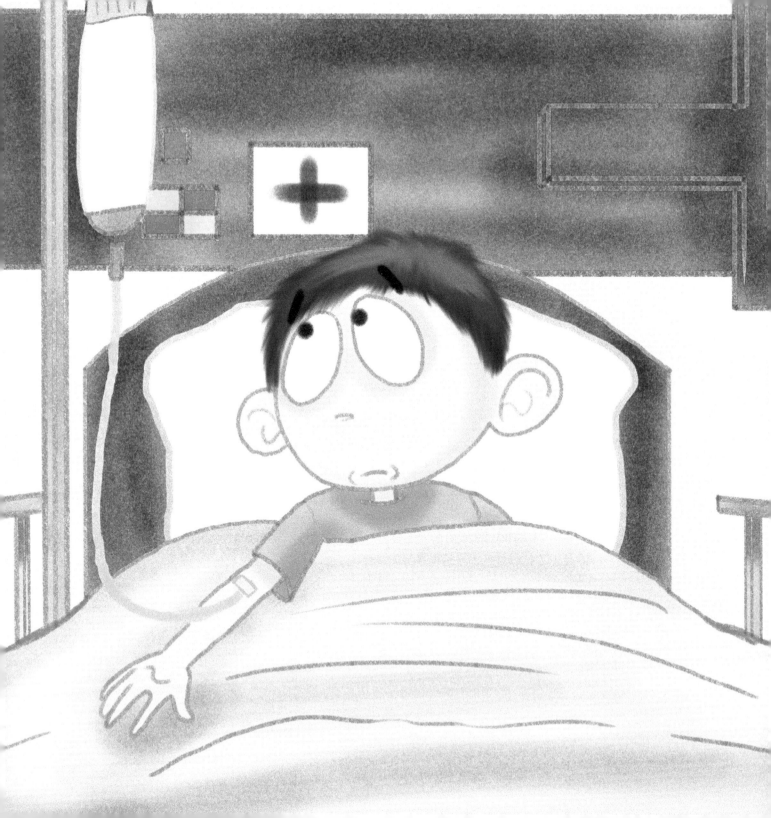

I started taking an antibiotic twice every day. Then, my parents and I flew all the way to Chicago, Illinois so I could have IVIg or *intravenous Immune globulin*.

A nurse put an IV in my arm to give me Immune globulin to help my immune system, over two days. IVIg helps your antibodies behave properly.

Then, your symptoms start to go away, most of the time. But, some kids need to have IVIg two or more times to really start getting better.

Boy, was I sick of having to take so much medicine and getting poked with needles.

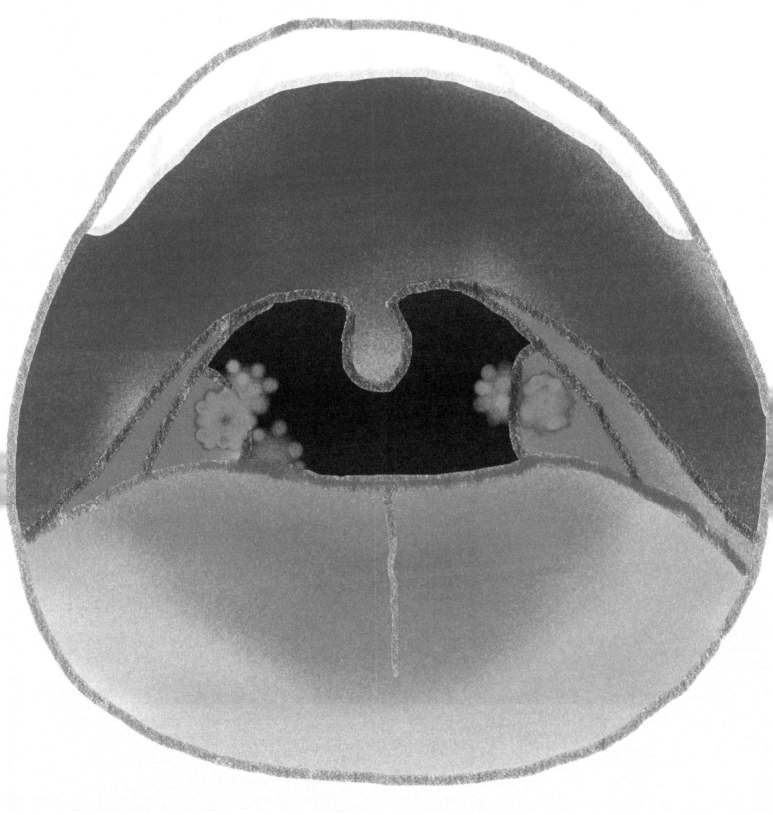

Some kids, like me, get their tonsils out, too. Tonsils are made of tissue and are located in the back of your throat on both sides.

Some doctors believe the bacteria hides inside or behind them, keeping you sick. Once they are out, you can start to get better.

But, you still need to take an antibiotic twice a week for awhile. It protects you just in case you are exposed to someone who is sick, like at school.

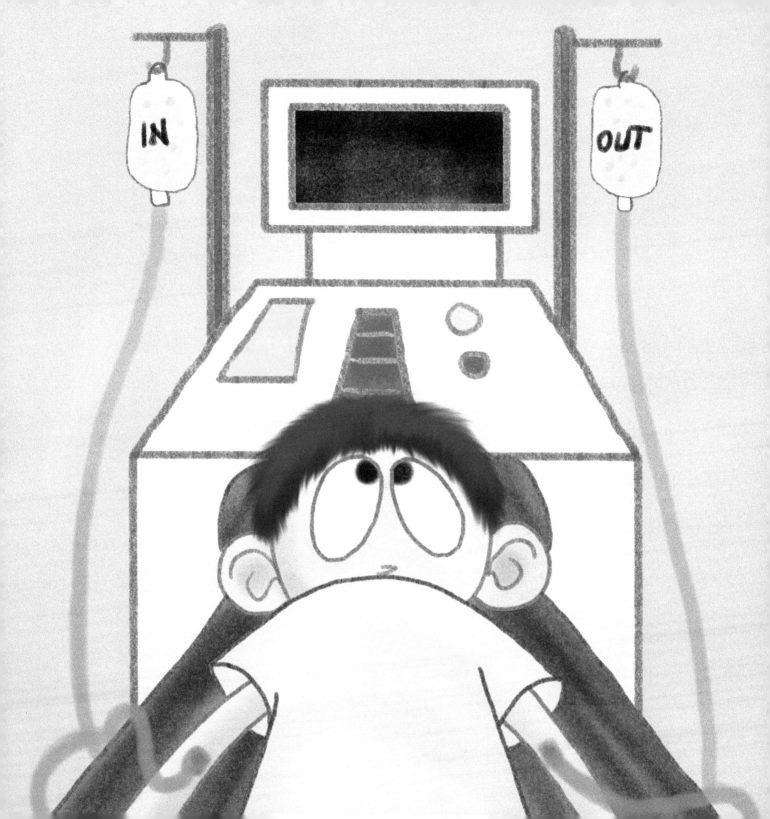

Another treatment is called *plasmapheresis*.

It's a procedure where the *plasma* in your blood gets taken out of you through a special machine to remove the antibodies that aren't working right.

Then, new plasma or something similar replaces what was taken out. This procedure takes about a week in the hospital to get it done right. But, don't worry, your parents can stay with you and the doctors and nurses will take really good care of you.

Once you start getting better, you start to feel normal and back to your old self again.

I was sick for several years with PANDAS because it took a long time for the doctors to figure out what was wrong and properly treat it.

If the doctor figures it out right away and you get an antibiotic right away, you won't be sick for very long or get so many symptoms.

PANDAS is not a very pleasant disorder. You have to just hang in there and let your parents and doctors do what they need to do to help you get better.

With proper treatment you *will* get better and be able to live a normal life. Before you know it, PANDAS will just be a thing in your past and you will forget all about it.

Then, the only pandas you might have in your life will be the black and white bears at the zoo!

Quotes

"I am only one, but still I am one. I cannot do everything, but still I can do something; and because I cannot do everything, I will not refuse to do the something that I can do."

-- Edward Everett Hale

"You are only just one person in this World, but you may be the World to just one person."

--Anonymous

"It is likely that following a century of unsuccessful search for the disease of the mind, the body will be where the answers shall be found."

--Miroslav Kovacevic, MD

GLOSSARY

Antibiotic: a drug used to kill bacteria and prevent disease

Antibodies: proteins in the blood that react to foreign proteins, neutralizing and producing immunity against them

Anxiety: an overwhelming feeling of uncertainty or nervousness

Autoimmune: when the immune system attacks one's own body

Bacteria: microorganisms that cause disease

Immune system: the body's 'army' of blood cells that fight infection or resist disease

Intravenous Immune globulin: a procedure that boosts your immune system by giving you donor Immune globulin or antibodies

Lyme: a disease caused by the Lyme tic

Mycoplasma: a bacteria that causes walking pneumonia

Obsessive Compulsive Disorder: persistent intrusive thoughts and/or repetitive movements

PANDAS: Pediatric Autoimmune Neuropsychiatric Disorder Associated with Streptococcus

PANS: Pediatric Acute-onset Neuropsychiatric Syndrome

Plasma: liquid portion of blood that contains antibodies

Plasmapheresis: a procedure that removes plasma from blood, which contains antibodies, and replaces it with donor plasma or a substitute

Streptococcus: bacteria that usually infects the throat or other areas, also referred to as strep

Symptoms: signs of change on the body's functions or appearance

Throat Culture: throat swab to determine presence of streptococcus

Tourette's Syndrome: tic disorder

Virus: any variety of microscopic organisms that cause disease that cannot be treated with antibiotics

Melanie S. Weiss, RNC-MNN, BSN has been a registered nurse for thirty years, certified in maternal-newborn nursing. Her goals in writing this book were to explain a frightening illness to the children afflicted with it, in an informative but non-frightening way, and to raise awareness about the disorder. She is also the author of the article, *"The Pandemonium of PANDAS."* Melanie lives on Long Island, NY with her husband and three sons and is an employee of the North Shore LIJ Health System.

*A portion of the proceeds from the sale of this book will go directly to PANDAS/PANS research through pandasnetwork.org.

Resources

pandasnetwork.org

nepandasparents.com

midwestpandas.com

webpediatrics.com

strepmonster.com

nimh.nih.gov

CPSIA information can be obtained
at www.ICGtesting.com
Printed in the USA
LVHW071507200219
608162LV00022B/1385/P